WASHING THE WINGS
OF THE ANGELS

OTHER WORK BY BOB HEMAN

Cone Transformed

The Number 5 Is Always Suspect
[*with Cindy Hochman*]

The House of Grand Farewells

As If

Acts of Innuendo

as much as you think you know

Assuming the Light

Lore

& Nothing More

[26 Structures]

what needs to be found

Demographics, or, The Hats
They Are Allowed to Wear

Recent Information

How It All Began

Something Snaps Its Fingers

Clues

Expecting Rain

Rosaries of Atoms

WASHING THE WINGS OF THE ANGELS

79 Pieces of Information

Bob Heman

A CLEARSOUND BOOK FROM
Quale Press

These pieces were previously published in *Otoliths*, *Calibanonline*, *First Literary Review-East*, *Muddy River Poetry Review*, *Home Planet News Online*, *DMQ Review* (*Disquieting Muses Quarterly*), *Unlikely Stories*, *Uut Poetry*, *Blazing Stadium*, *Clockwise Cat*, *Forum of World Cultures*, *Levure Litteraire*, *No Placebos*, *Poetrybay*, *Public Illumination*, *Right Hand Pointing*, *Upstairs at Duroc*, and in the single-author issue of *The Moron Channel* titled *disparate works*. They have been anthologized in *Alcatraz* (Life Before Man, 2022), *Escape Wheel* (great weather for MEDIA, 2020), and *A Shape Produced by a Curve* (great weather for MEDIA, 2023), as well as in the annual *Brevitas* and *Brownstone Poets* anthologies. A few are also posted on the *Brevitas* website.

Copyright © 2024 by Bob Heman
ISBN: 978-1-935835-33-2 trade paperback edition
LCCN: 2024932929

Collages by the author: *Arriving* (cover), *The First Encounter* (page vii), *Calling the Angels* (page 81)

Interior and cover design by Alex Greulich

A ClearSound book from
Quale Press
www.quale.com

*Dedicated to the memory
of my old friend
Steve Fairhurst (1945–2009)
who founded Clown War with me
in the early 1970s*

AUTHOR'S NOTE

These pieces are part of my ongoing "information" series to which I have been adding since 1997. The pieces included here were written between 2014 and 2022 and are arranged in the order in which they were written.

When I have performed the pieces publicly, or have published them individually, I have preceded each with the generic title "INFORMATION." Here, instead of giving them each that generic title, I've chosen to omit the titles, instead capitalizing the first few words of each piece.

CONTENTS

WAITS FOR	1
HAS TO BE	2
PRACTICE SAYING	3
IN THE SPRING	4
HAS TO START	5
THEY TOLD	6
THE MACHINE	7
THERE WERE	8
LISTENS FOR	9
MEASURES HIS	10
IN 1934	11
MOST OF THEM	12
ASSEMBLED	13
IN THE POEM	14
SIMPLE MATH	15
ONE CAN	16
THERE WERE	17
SOMEONE WHO	18
AT NIGHT	19
NOT EVERY	20
EACH NEW	21

IN THE MOVIE	22
IN CERTAIN	23
HE FELT	24
LOOKS FOR	25
THE CIRCLE	26
"CONEY ISLAND"	27
IN THIS GAME	28
OF COURSE	29
ONE CAN USE	30
SEWS THE EARS	31
WE MUST	32
WASHING	33
IT IS NOT	34
THE SYMBOLS	35
BELIEVE THIS:	36
A PLOT	37
SOME OF	38
THE KIDS YELLING	39
AFTER YOU DIE	40
SHE DID NOT	41
CONFUSES	42
AT THIS POINT	43
THE SPECIAL	44

THE SONG	45
CONFUSES ADAM	46
CONFUSES GOD	47
IT IS ABOUT	48
PERPETUATES	49
A POEM WITHOUT	50
SHE KNEW	51
THEY WILL EAT	52
ONE STORY	53
NO MATTER	54
LISTEN CLOSELY	55
SEES SOMETHING	56
THE PAPER BOATS	57
IF THERE ARE	58
THEIR BODIES	59
THEY DID NOT	60
THEY SIT	61
IS TAUGHT	62
CONTINUITY REQUIRES	63
IT IS A SPECIAL	54
LEARNS TO SAY	65
SIGNIFICANT DETAILS	66
THE MUSIC	67

I WANT	68
IF THE BASIC	69
IT'S NOT	70
REWIND. TO WHERE	71
HE WAS LOOKING	72
THE DEATH	73
REMEMBERS HOW	74
THE HEART	75
WHAT WAS HIDDEN	76
STOLE FIRE	77
THE OBJECT	78
IS ABLE	79

WAITS FOR the words to arrive, but there are no words, only birds circling around, large birds, gulls, too far inland to be normal, as if fleeing the storm the words would certainly bring if they could ever be found.

HAS TO BE like the story was, meandering a bit, with no destination in mind. He didn't know there'd be bears. He didn't know there'd be a boat, or a hat filled with bees. He expected choices, but not the choices he was given. Everything changed when the woman spoke. Everything changed when the car wouldn't start.

PRACTICE SAYING "thank you." Practice saying "the cat is dead." Practice saying "there are not enough." Practice saying "use the red road." Practice saying "where is the woman?" Practice saying "there's too much lemon."

IN THE SPRING the owls bloomed and the wheels turned more slowly. In the spring the woman's hair reached all the way to the sea. In the spring there were bears singing and a tree that finally opened its eyes.

HAS TO START the machine that makes the bears cute and the machine that rearranges the cabin. Has to start with a list of the cows that are no longer red. Has to start with the man who has only just learned how to count. Has to start with some dirt inside of a hat. Has to start with a word that was broken in half. Has to start with some frogs that were rusted.

THEY TOLD the machine about the bears and the machine showed them a picture of a kaleidoscope. They told the machine about the mountain and the machine showed them the picture of a box of crayons. The machine became two machines and then four and then eight. Each was given a number that had no other meaning.

THE MACHINE told them to listen. It told them to replace their bodies with a house in the woods. It told them to replace the bears with the word "octagon." It told them to wear clothes made out of moss.

THERE WERE no more pictures of blackboards, no more chairs made of rope, no more stories about the punishment strap, no more women filled with whispers, no more doilies shaped like bears, no more cars that had to be wound up.

LISTENS FOR something he calls music, but it is only the wind, the birds, the breakers. When it is given these names it is no longer recognized.

MEASURES HIS arm, and his head, and his penis. Measures how much water his lungs will hold. Measures the trees that are behind him and the distance to the map. Measures the space the woman must occupy.

IN 1934 the bears were replaced with a penguin and an ant. In 1952 the line was doubled in length. In 1967 the color red was added.

MOST OF THEM did not know that there would be punishment in heaven as well.

ASSEMBLED the circus from the machines that were left in the ocean, from the machines that remained in the empty lot, from the machines that had been used to rearrange the dead. Used animals that were incomplete and trees that were incorrectly drawn. Used a truck that they called the ringmaster to lift the tent higher than the stars. Used clowns that were really only boxes of baling wire, and elephants that resembled ears of corn.

IN THE POEM the bear was shaped like a mailbox, the woman like a cup full of salt. In the poem the dirt spoke more quickly than they could understand. In the poem they were the dirt, the bear, the woman, but when they were opened the numbers that spilled out were different from what they had expected. They had no meaning that corresponded with any truth.

SIMPLE MATH is always a lie. Two bicycles and two cows never add up to more than a single umbrella.

ONE CAN compare a potato chip with a spanking or a cloud with a paper bag. Every metaphor began as a lie, and every lie as an ocean that was better forgotten.

THERE WERE several ways to build birds. Only one of them used an egg, and that was the egg of a lizard.

SOMEONE WHO does not know the value of words, the value of 2+3, the value of the color green, the value of the clouds hidden beneath the ocean, the value of the first words the woman ever learned, the value of the bear substituted for the three travelers, the value of the idea of systematic discipline, the value of the car shaped like a frog, the value of the road on the map that corresponded to no real road, the value of speculative truths, the value of the rain.

AT NIGHT the streets cross more frequently.

NOT EVERY poem has a butterfly or a rose, or a man who must be taught how to sing. Sometimes machines have replaced the ocean, and the birds are made of paper. The road they follow is the only road they are allowed to see.

EACH NEW language began with a mistake, a word misheard or misspelled, a phrase that pointed in the wrong direction, a speaker who became the spoken about, a color that became too deep to climb out of, a structure that was too parallel to ever be counted, an animal that was mistaken for a pronoun, a woman whose location could not be described.

IN THE MOVIE the body weighs more than soap, more than the bouquet of orchids, more than the telescope filled with hamsters. In the movie the body is carried down the stairs to the place where the pool is beginning to breathe, to the place where the men resemble barnacles, to the place where the woman has been wrongly assembled. Each time the stars arrive a different word is released from the frog that has begun to resemble.

IN CERTAIN climates the apple becomes a boat, the cat becomes a door, each fern grows higher than the hat made of ice. In June the ketchup limps up the mountain, never occupying the place the question requires. The separate toes are usually very wet, an "x" the body has yet to deposit in the zone of explanations.

HE FELT as good as dirt, as incomplete as an octopus, as nervous as the word "diameter," as sullen as a box full of tangos. His only name was "distance," his only dimension a mirror, his only explanation a radish that was burning. He was repeated but never restored. Only sometimes was he allowed a circle.

LOOKS FOR a metaphor that contains only women, that contains a car with rusted wheels and the word "pontoon." Looks for a metaphor that must be deflated before it can be used. Looks for a metaphor that has been repeated too many times, and a metaphor that contains only unfamiliar numbers. Looks for a metaphor that is a rearrangement, and must be followed off of the page.

THE CIRCLE, the square, and the triangle are the first tools they are given. The second tool is perspective, and the third is color. The image only comes later, either drawn to resemble, or formed of words that suggest what cannot be drawn.

"CONEY ISLAND" is only sometimes the answer. At other times the answer is "iguana" or "Warren G. Harding."

IN THIS GAME there are only stones or beans, and a box used for sorting or counting. We are asked to imagine the bees even though we have never seen them. We are asked to imagine the bears and their amazement at finding the sea. We are asked to imagine what the horizon might really be. We are told to record our journeys even though all we do is follow the only line we are given. Sometimes the game is played on a map. Or in places where there is no light.

OF COURSE, the peasants are dancing. It helps them to forget the dead, the mutilated bodies found in the pastures where the cattle are afraid to go. The tower is all that remains of the castle that once cast its shadow across the entire land. There were rumors, of course, but they stopped each time the trains approached, each time the full moon screamed across the night sky, each time the animals were discovered to be only frayed puppets, moved unceasingly by unseen hands.

ONE CAN USE bacon as a metaphor, can remove it from the menu, can use it to threaten the children. Each time its explanation is no more than an animal that is almost forgotten, no more than a hunger they have never been able to sate, no more than a lesson in the construction of a sturdy home. They know that salt is only one of the machines necessary for its fabrication. They know its name can only be spoken in nightmares.

SEWS THE EARS back onto the cow. Forces it to read a magazine about machinery. Permits it to wander into the forest where the river cannot reach. Calls it by the name that has been painted on its side. Allows it to be portrayed by a bear in the movie of its life.

WE MUST learn the bulldozer and the tractor and the dump truck. We must learn the fire engine. We must learn the tugboat and the circus train. We must learn the giraffe and the bullfrog. We must learn the polar bear. We must learn the dragonfly and the praying mantis. We must learn the game of Monopoly and the game of checkers. We must learn the sky and the forest. We must learn the color red. We must learn about death.

WASHING the wings of the dragonflies is nothing at all like washing the wings of the angels. It's not just the color and texture that differs, but the light that rubs off on your hands.

IT IS NOT magic if the doll is pulled by a string. It is not the stars that move—it is us. Sometimes the sea gives back its dead. Sometimes the word that is required is a word older than the sea itself. If it is mispronounced the results will not be the same.

THE SYMBOLS they were given included nuns dancing with each other, rabbits constructed out of barbed wire, a child's doll designed by Hans Bellmer. There were doors that could not be entered. There was also a box that had once been a cactus, and a man who was really a swimming fish.

BELIEVE THIS: men have walked on the moon. Believe this: the water is boiling. Believe this: you will not remember what they said. Believe this: you have not always been alone. Believe this: the birds once were dinosaurs. Believe this: there are more words that have not yet found you.

A PLOT that has no bears is no kind of plot at all. It's not enough to have the color red and the number 5. It's not enough to have a man and a woman who may, or may not, like each other. It's not enough that it be raining all the time, or that the windows cannot be opened.

SOME OF the generic children wear glasses, or are overweight. Some of them have learned words that are three or four letters long. Some of them will eat broccoli, but not cantaloupe. Some of them say their prayers, but have still been punished. Some of them think they can find the light that they see in their dreams. Some of them have heard whispers that seem to call their names. Sometimes they have answered them.

THE KIDS YELLING "easy out" never saw the star that filled the sky behind them, never saw the rodent that limped across the outfield grass, never saw the woman who was no more than a shadow of what was to come. Their game was an exception to the wrong turns their lives were given, an exception to the distance that led them back to where they began.

AFTER YOU DIE they will dig you up and make you labor in the sugar mill. After you die you will have wings you never had before. After you die, for the first time, you will know how to swim. After you die you will speak words that will change those who hear them. After you die you will finally understand love.

SHE DID NOT know if her story should be classified as "true crime" or "romance" or "natural science." She did not know if the title should be printed in red ink or blue. She did not know if there would ever be a sequel. She did not know if anyone would ever read it out loud.

CONFUSES the roll of paper towels with William Bendix. Counts the leaves as they fall from the tree. It is safe to assume she has her own agenda, one which includes the castle that intrudes on the horizon and the idea of the sleep that always avoids her. She is not who they think she is, but their description of her is still accurate.

AT THIS POINT in the plot she twists her ankle, he watches the owls, the car runs out of gas. At this point in the plot the railroad tracks curve out of sight, the notices posted on the power pole take on a new meaning, the dogs cry like babies. At this point the trees become an exception, the room a mistake that gives them hope. At this point they are taught the truth about the sky.

THE SPECIAL effects can make you seem larger or smaller, older or younger, or more attractive than you have ever been. They can give you an arm that is mechanical, or a mind full of tentacles, or a room full of children that have been assembled from plastic. They can turn you into a bear that they all recognize at once, just before they gather around the table for supper.

THE SONG about the old gray mare had nothing to do with the discovery of radium. The man dressed in pajamas was not the same man once his outline was revealed. The elephants would always be the wrong kind of explanation. Still, they were mentioned far too often.

CONFUSES ADAM and Eve with Dick and Jane. Confuses Santa Claus with god, and the tree with a loving uncle. Confuses the sky with the ocean they are afraid to wade in. Confuses the fingers they count on with the explanation for goulash.

CONFUSES GOD with Satan, even though their plans are not the same. Thinks the word that is said is the only word that can be said. Understands that the forest is only a response to the sky, that the man is only a response to the woman. Is left alone to think about these things.

IT IS ABOUT the experience that it gives you. That is its meaning. The mailbox filled with popcorn is no more than that. It is the reason there are pockets. The reason that you are able to find a voice in the forest, in the ocean, in the animal that is always silent. The reason there is counting long after there is nothing more to count.

PERPETUATES the image of the chicken crossing the road, of monkeys eating bananas, of a bear dancing in the costume of a gypsy. Perpetuates the use of the word "meaning" in such situations, even when it is not appropriate, even when the word "representation" would be more correct.

A POEM WITHOUT adjectives. A poem without adverbs. A poem without numbers or colors or women carrying baskets. A poem without bicycles. A poem without diagrams or windows that cannot be opened. A poem without a woman whose hair is no more than a metaphor. A poem without frogs or bears. A poem without meaning. A poem that is never old enough to cast a shadow.

SHE KNEW it was fun to make mommy chase her, but she didn't know enough words yet to make it real. The dog and the bird and the cat inhabited her world and spoke to her while she slept. The more familiar the trees became the more they scared her. She put on her green dress when she was happy.

THEY WILL EAT the dead. They will eat their own hands. They will eat the machines that look like trees, and the water that trickles out of the sky. They will eat the dreams that might have saved them, and the words that try to explain it all. They will eat the future even before it is able to arrive.

ONE STORY ends with fire, or with water, or with a man falling through the air. Another ends with a woman digging in the earth, searching for a different way for the story to end. Each time a man appears he is a different man, wearing a different suit of clothes. Each time a woman enters she is the same woman, always asking the same question over and over again. Sometimes an animal is required to end the story in an appropriate way.

NO MATTER how much she tugged on his ears they didn't get any larger. The history of forsythias never included what happened next. It was not true that she changed into salt.

LISTEN CLOSELY and you will hear the moans of the damned. Listen closely and you will hear animals singing the songs of the angels. Listen closely and you will hear the horizon approaching. Listen closely and you will hear your own body losing its last breath. Listen closely and then repeat everything that you have heard.

SEES SOMETHING different on the map than he is intended to see. He thinks the road is a river, and the cluster of buildings a place to disembark. The length of the river depends only on where the map ends or begins. There are places where he must make decisions he is not yet able to make. He does not know how the journey will end. He does not know what is hidden in the section marked "forest."

THE PAPER BOATS confuse the bears. They are not large enough to get inside, and have no motors so they can only drift with the currents. The bears don't realize that the boats are very much like the bears themselves, who never understand their own reason for being, and who frequently lack the motivation to leave their caves, even after spring has approached.

IF THERE ARE stairs the narrative will be taken to the second floor. Or down into the cellar where something that is sleeping waits to be awakened. There are windows that cannot be opened, and others that cannot be closed. There is a door that is only the replica of a door, and a mannequin that resembles the man who stands silently on their lawn. It is only when the dog barks that the moon starts to approach. It is only then that the meaning of the caption becomes obvious.

THEIR BODIES will become a feast for crocodiles, and only then the subject for a poem. Each time the sun returns a different victim's body is discovered. The poems created in this way will be brittle and terse, and filled with no more imagination than the reader brings to them. Weakness of the heart never becomes a factor, nor does the shortness of breath the poem is likely to elicit.

THEY DID NOT know yet if the man in pajamas would be the killer or the killed. The train schedule said the next stop would be Wolfshead, and not Sheepdip as announced. The weapon used had to be something unexpected, like a corkscrew, or a noun. When the woman spoke all the adjectives gathered around her to listen. She was subject to the usual rules of usage, but somehow she twisted them to her own advantage.

THEY SIT at their machines that have no moving parts, that have more in common with candles than with vacuum cleaners or pencil sharpeners or automobiles. They have not yet discovered the language that will be necessary for them to communicate. They have not yet discovered the sequence of commands that will enable them to control their future. They were given a set of assumptions that are no longer relevant, and a door that can no longer be opened. Each time they open their eyes they must learn it all again.

IS TAUGHT how to use the key, the ruler, the glass. Is taught how to count the woman's steps, and how to count his own. His first word described the cat, and the water in the bowl. The second word described their absence, as well as his own absence from the future that was not yet his own. Opening the door did not change what was on the other side. But closing it did.

CONTINUITY REQUIRES that the flashlight always be held in his left hand, that the woman always be wearing only one shoe, that the owl be removed each time the coach passes. It requires that the words always be spoken in Hungarian, and that each one always be a verb. It requires that the woman be never more than an explanation, and that only the color red be used.

IT IS A SPECIAL kind of erotica that includes a window, an owl, a basket full of washers. A special kind that asks you to repeat a single word again and again, that asks the woman to resume her counting, that never wants you to watch.

LEARNS TO SAY "what the fuck" in response to certain situations. Learns to count anything that can be repeated. Learns the difference between the cow and the drawing of the cow. Learns the difference between the sky and the mirror. Knows that the words have a different purpose that she hasn't yet discovered. Learns that she is only half of the story.

SIGNIFICANT DETAILS remembered later on: a man made of straw, a car that was broken, a trail that led deeper than they wanted to go. They spoke about distance when they meant the diameter, and dinner when they meant the dawn. Each word they spoke corresponded with a different clue. There was always a woman waiting, but they were never sure what she was waiting for.

THE MUSIC was the wrong size to fit inside of the plot. Even if its head was shaved and its spurs removed it still would not fit. They had to cajole it so it would stay at all. But it was the only mirror they could find to use. It grew angry if its tail was touched, or if it was imitated by the poultry. It grew angry too if it was given a name too soon. No one could be found who could understand its branches, or the things that grew there. There was no one who could measure it without allowing its fluids to escape.

I WANT no credit that isn't due me. I want the moon only if it is permitted. I want the color green when it isn't alive and the color blue when it is. I want a word that can be repeated without changing. I want a woman who didn't just happen, and an animal that wasn't just drawn on. I want to be folded into your dreams.

IF THE BASIC plot doesn't work, you can always add quicksand, or a tree that doesn't cast a shadow.

IT'S NOT the bracelet we're supposed to notice, but the scars on her wrists. The distance between her arms the only distance she will ever travel. The song she is supposed to sing does not advance the plot. When she exits stage right she understands that the bear will follow.

REWIND. TO WHERE the bird is flying overhead, to where the woman seems to have two bodies, to where the forest is only starting to burn. Rewind. And then rewind again. So that the sun is repeated, so that the moon is broken, so that the man escapes from the only label he has been given. Each time we watch we will have new thoughts, but never enough to escape from the prison we call our bodies.

HE WAS LOOKING for a cloud he saw in a movie when he was a child. He was looking for the car that whizzed by him in a dream. He was trying to remember the words he overheard outside his parents' bedroom. He was trying to remember the shadows the picket fence cast. He was trying to remember when it all began.

THE DEATH of the father repeated in the movement of objects, in the counting of waves, in the reassembling of shadows into something that is almost familiar.

REMEMBERS HOW to write, remembers how to kiss, remembers how to count, remembers the difference between the bumble bee and the hummingbird, between the color red and the number 5, between the man and the woman, between the sky at night and the sky in the morning, between the hand when it is open and the hand when it is closed.

THE HEART can sometimes be repaired with thread and a curved needle such as sail-makers use. But its ability to love in the future can never be guaranteed.

WHAT WAS HIDDEN no more than a space where the air could be held and measured, a space where the light never reached unless a lamp were lit, a space where the men and women gathered waiting to be bathed or fed. It was a space where the stories began, where the river was constructed from the rain that was left over, where bread had been invented as a substitute for the apples and pears that grew increasingly rare. It was a space where written words were first pronounced and shared, a space where a drawing on the wall was thought to be the same as the animal it portrayed, a space where music filled the corners until there was no longer a place to hide.

STOLE FIRE from the blacksmith and fire from the baker and fire from the woman who tended the altar. Stole water from the machine that created the lake and earth from the place where the priests were buried. Stole air from the lungs of the tired horse. Stole a tree that never grew old and a snake that spoke only lies. Stole books from the well where they had been hidden and a bowl from the museum of promises. Stole the caption that would have let this all make sense and the number that gave it a place in time. Stole the only name by which it would be known.

THE OBJECT represents the wind, represents the journey that is always no more than a circle that has not been closed.

IS ABLE to count using dice or coins or a spinning wheel. Is able to count using the word "hesitate" or the color red. Is able to count using the man and the woman, using the abandoned silo, using the roads on the map that do not cross. Is able to count, and to use those numbers to resist the lure of the mirror. Is able to count until it is no longer his turn.

quale [kwä-lay]. *Eng. n 1.* A property (such as hardness) considered apart from things that have that property. 2. A property that is experienced as distinct from any source it may have in a physical object. *Ital. pron. a.* 1. Which, what. 2. Who. 3. Some. 4. As, just as.

www.ingramcontent.com/pod-product-compliance
Lightning Source LLC
Chambersburg PA
CBHW030959090426
42737CB00007B/606